100

HIGH-PERFORMING
SOCIAL MEDIA AD COPIES
FOR REALTORS

A Real Estate Marketing Playbook: 100 Ready-To-Use
Ad Copies for Real Estate Agents & Brokers To
Generate More Leads From Facebook & Instagram

Nick Tsai

High-Performing Real Estate Email Campaigns for Realtors by Nick Tsai

Published by Wishstone Trading Limited

Https://soldouthouses.com

Copyright © 2022 Nick Tsai

BONUSES

Bonus 1- Special Discount For 360 Social Media Ad Templates

Start creating appealing ad images with our 360 social media ad images templates
Claim your special discount at http://soldouthouses.com/adtemplates/

Bonus 2- The Ultimate Real Estate Marketing Checklist

This checklist features 86 marketing tips to generate more leads online & offline.

Download your free checklist at https://soldouthouses.com/checklist

Bonus 3- 10X Leadgen Virtual Bootcamp (Free Training)

Join our online Bootcamp to learn how you can generate
more leads online with digital marketing, sign up now at:
https://soldouthouses.com/10xleadgenbootcamp

TABLE OF CONTENTS

INTRODUCTION

Thanks for getting the book.

You made a smart decision because in this short publication, you will discover the ads that are working for both our clients and our business.

And unlike many copywriting materials, this book doesn't teach you how to write copy. Even though it's an essential skill, it normally takes someone years to master the art of copywriting.

So instead, we published this book as a done-for-you toolkit that you can literally copy and paste and use right away.

The ad copy featured in this book is all written by my team members and professional copywriters. Our clients have had great results with it.

If you have been in the real estate industry for a while, you know how competitive it is. And to stand out in the crowd, you must be extraordinary in every aspect of your marketing and selling.

Luckily, you don't have to fight alone. I published this short book and founded Soldouthouses.com to help real estate professionals generate more leads and close more sales without spending lots of money.

Since this may be your first purchase from me, I want to introduce myself with the hope you'll feel like you can trust me.

Who Am I?

Hi, my name is Nick Tsai. I'm a digital marketing expert with over 10 years of marketing experience.

Ten years ago, I was a realtor. As a rookie, I struggled to get clients even though I followed the traditional advice from the industry:

- Distributing flyers
- Posting classified ads
- Cold calling
- Cold mailing

But nothing worked for me.

I was frustrated, tired of struggling, and hopeless. I worked 12-hour days every day and still got no clients. I eventually burned out and quit. I lost my confidence, and self-doubt crept in.

Those were the worst days of my life.

Then one day, I received a phone call that changed everything.

It was from a stranger who wanted me to help him sell this house.

I had never called or mailed him and didn't even know who he was.

But, for some reason, he found my website.

It was an ugly blog I used as a personal notebook where I wrote down everything I learned about real estate.

For some strange reason, it became my local area's #1 ranking real estate blog.

In the next few months, people kept calling. They asked me about real estate and even begged to be taken on as clients.

All of a sudden, I became the go-to expert in the local area.

And getting clients became effortless.

It was an "aha" moment, and I realized "It's easier to attract clients than to chase them."

In the past, I pursued potential clients by cold calling, mailing, and sending flyers (aka junk mail). I became an annoying salesperson.

But by harnessing the power of the internet, I can easily reach people ready to buy and position myself as an expert!

So, I decided to dive into internet marketing to discover how I could attract more clients online. I studied countless marketing books, attended marketing seminars, and learned from the best marketing experts in the world.

And that's why I set up Soldouthouses.com so realtors like I once was can get results with digital marketing.

HOW TO USE THIS BOOK

This book provides 100 real estate ad copies that have been proven and are working well for our real estate clients.

All the copies in this book are written for social media ads, which means you can easily plug in and play for your social media marketing.

You can either copy and paste these ad copies, customize them for your business or create ad images for them.

And if you want to use them on an image-based social media platform, such as Facebook or Instagram, you definitely need to create ad images for them; I highly recommend Canva - powerful free software that helps you get the job done quickly.

Also, if you are too busy to create ad images, **my team has put together a special package of 360 social media ad templates that you can easily drag and drop to create professional ad images.**

You can go to http://soldouthouses.com/adtemplates/ to check them out and get all of them for a special discount.

DONE-FOR-YOU AD COPY

Dream Home Buyers Ads

The right ad copy can catch the eye of potential buyers looking for their dream home. But for most, not overspending is on their minds too. They are more likely to engage when given a chance to get the right place at the right price. The ads should be used when targeting home buyers across various categories.

A similar recent campaign produced brilliant results, displayed here, where 31 leads were generated at an average of $1,500 each.

Similarly, 21 leads were created for $2.59 with 3322 impressions, which is a very good number. This implies that 3322 individuals saw this ad, and the reach and results of the campaign can be regarded as a success for only a few dollars.

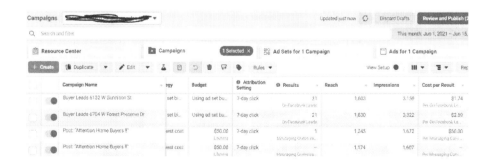

Dream Home Buyers Ad Copy

Ad copy 1

Headline: Buy a home without the risk of overpaying for the property🏠🏠.

Primary text: For property buyers, it is an inherent risk that they might overpay for a property. If you lack knowledge about the current market rates, don't worry. You can avoid overpaying just by contacting the right people at ….

Ad copy 2

Headline: Finding your dream house will not be easy even if you have the resources😮🏠!

Primary text: Yes, you read it right. Even if you have the money, you might still be unable to find your dream home. There could be multiple reasons why that is so. Better your chances of finding your dream home with the help of an expert.

Ad copy 3

Headline: 😍😍🏠🏠Own the luxurious home you have always desired. Click here for more information.

Primary text: Having your entire family together at a luxurious house is desired by many. But there are multiple buyers for these amazing houses that are for sale now. Do not miss out on the opportunity of owning a luxurious house in____ city.

Ad copy 4

Headline: Stunning homes for sale. Don't miss the opportunity to own one👍.

Primary text: The best deals don't last long, and the best options sell quickly. Check out the list of amazing homes we have for you right now. Don't miss the opportunity of owning your dream home.

Ad copy 5

Headline: Your perfect ___city home search starts here 👆

Primary text: 🔥🔥🔥The market is heating up in _____. There is an overwhelming number of Star homes for your family. But setting the filters right and finding what you really need can be a challenge. Log onto our website and make your search for the perfect home in ___ so much simpler.

!

Ad copy 6

Headline: Finding a place called home😃😃👨‍👩‍👧🏠🏠!

Primary text: So many of us settle for less than what we deserve when calling a place home. And it's not always due to a lack of options in the market or our resources. Rather, we don't look in the right places and don't seek the expert help at the right time. Get in touch with us. Let us help you find a place you can call home.

Ad copy 7

Headline: 😎✌️✌️✌️We simplify the process of buying a new home for you. Get in touch with us at www.___

Primary text: There is great excitement at the prospect of moving into a bigger and better space. But joy can be short-lived because of the challenges that come with finding a new home that ticks all the boxes. You can make that process smoother and easier by contacting us at...

Ad copy 8

Headline: 😵 😵 😵 🎯 🎯 🎯 Attention potential homebuyers in ___ city: The time to invest is now.

Primary text: If you are looking to own a house in ___ city, then you must act swiftly as the market is favorable for buyers. Don't miss this amazing opportunity by making the wrong choices. Get in touch with us at www. ___ to learn more about your best options right now.

Ad copy 9

Headline: 🏠❤️ Get a real estate pro on your side!

Primary text: Buying a home is not simple, especially for first-time homeowners who lack experience with the process. Several questions may be ringing in your head about loans, mortgage payments, cash issues, taxation and so much more. But having a real estate professional by your side helps with all of it.

Ad copy 10

Headline: 💲🏠🙋 ☐ What's stopping you from owning that amazing home you always desired?

Primary text: If you have the funds for the down payment and the willingness to purchase a new property, maybe it's not having the right real estate professional by your side that's slowing you down. Get the best real estate solutions at www. ___ and make the process of buying that new home so much easier.

Off-Market Buyers Ads

These ads target buyers who are looking for off-market properties. With off-market properties not listed on multiple platforms, it provides the buyers with much-needed time. And with less competition and hustling going on, they are likely to make better decisions. This should attract buyers who are not willing to jump into a bidding war. This can be used when both the buyers and sellers want to avoid the mainstream channels and maintain privacy. I have attached results from a similar campaign run not that long ago. The statistics show us the importance of a well-targeted ad campaign. Although 24 results at an average cost of $6.24 cannot be classified as the cheapest, the cost depends on many things. The specified target market also affects the average cost per result, but getting 29 leads under $10 is a very presentable outcome.

Off-Market Buyers Ad Copy

Ad copy 11

Headline: 🌐 💲 🏠 Less clutter, more opportunities. Check out the best off-market listings at our website right now.

Primary text: A lot of sellers prefer off-market sales. That also has benefits for the buyers. For the sellers, there is privacy; for the buyers, there is the opportunity to make an informed and calm decision. Check out the best off-market deals at our private listing by logging on to our website.

Ad copy 12

Headline: 👀 👀 The best off-market deals few know about in ____ city.

Primary text: An abundance of amazing properties go unnoticed and sell off-market. Don't be skeptical about sellers who won't list their properties on a number of platforms. There are plenty of valid reasons they choose not to list. For a buyer, there are advantages too. For the best off-market homes listings in ____ city, you can log on to www.____

Ad copy 13

Headline: 💧 💲 Attention! Are you looking to buy a home in ____ city under $500,000?

Primary text: Home buyers in ____ city can get lost in the clutter if they don't look in the right places. Log on to our website to see listings and check out the off-market listings as well. This can improve your chances of getting a good deal quicker.

Ad copy 14

Headline: 😎😍Get an exclusive list of homes in ___ Town. Log on to our website right now!

Primary text: When you contact us, we want you to feel like our only customer. Well, maybe you won't be, but just by filling out a form using our filters, you can get customized options of what you've been looking for. So, don't waste another moment. Log on to our website and check out the exclusive listings.

Ad copy 15

Headline: 😲👀❤Real estate investors get creative with off-market deals.

Primary text: The investment market is red hot right now. With low mortgage rates and people moving because of remote work, there is an influx of investors. Those who have limited or moderate experience with buying homes will find it hard to score the best deal in multiple listing services. We provide the best off-market deals at www._____

Listing Ad

This ad copy appeals to homebuyers who have an idea of how difficult the negotiations and paperwork are. They prefer to have a professional realtor to avoid the headache of doing it all alone. They will likely get through the listing knowing that a professional agent is aware of the entire process and has the authority from the principal as well. This works when potential buyers want to avoid the headache of lengthy negotiations. The statistics displayed here prove that the buyers were willing to engage when provided with what they wanted. This is proven by the campaign we ran from Dec 21-Jan 22 where we had a greater reach and impressions, which resulted in 37 lead generations in the first phase at an average cost of $3.02. Of these, 34 leads were generated at a higher cost of $8.04. But when the targeted audience was narrowed and very specific, an overall 71 lead generations for buyers only made this campaign a success.

Listing Ad Copy

Ad copy 16

Headline: 😎 🙌 ✓ You dream & we deliver!

Primary text: It becomes so much more convenient for the buyers if the listing agreements are in place between the principal and the agent. You don't have to wait for that to happen. At www.____ , you can check the listings right now and make the process of buying your dream home so much quicker.

Ad copy 17

Headline: 👪 🏠 ☑ Perfect family homes with locations that have easy access to just about everything!

Primary text: For those looking for the perfect family homes in ___, check out the listings at www.____ . Make the process of finding the best home easier for yourself. The professionals know how to navigate through the transaction perfectly.

Ad copy 18

Headline: 👆 🤝 🔍 Find the best deals in our listings by logging on to our website www.____ .

Primary text: For potential homebuyers in ___ city, there is no shortage of listings. But not everyone can match the options for you. Whether you are looking for a luxurious home or a modest one, we have a deal for everyone. Get in touch with us at www.____ .

Ad copy 19

Headline: 💲 🏠 ✓ 🌐 Check the listings for luxurious homes in ___ city at our website www.____ .

Primary text: As a potential homebuyer, you are likely to get more options at our website. We have compiled a list for you and have authority from the seller to take the negotiations forward. That makes a swift deal more likely. Log on to our website for fresh listings in ___ city.

Ad copy 20

Headline: [NEW] 👆 🏷️ ❤ Click to see our fresh listings that many will miss. Log on to our website right now.

Primary text: Sellers who are willing to pay the fee and get proper value for their homes list with trusted realtors. For buyers, that can mean the best properties are listed. So, it is worthwhile to invest time and look often at the listings. Our fresh listings have some amazing options, and you can check them at www.___ .

Seller Ads

Sellers don't have an easy ride when trying to get fair offers for their property. One problem is when their personal information like email and phone numbers are in the market and their privacy is compromised. Listing with a professional realtor takes care of that issue, which is why many sellers engage when selling their home. This can be used when targeting homeowners seeking to sell homes without the headache. Campaigns we ran just a few weeks ago brought decent results and continue to bring results. As shown here, a very recent campaign brought four leads in a very short time. While the campaign is still up and running and the cost per result could fall drastically, it is still not bad at $12.33 for four seller leads in the current market.

Sellers Ad Copy

Ad copy 21

Headline: 💲💸💸 Want to sell your home? Learn all about the correct valuation here.

Primary text: Everyone wants a good return on investment. But when it comes to selling a home at the best price, not everyone gets it right. If you are thinking about cashing in on the rising valuation of your home, then you have come to the perfect place.

Ad copy 22

Headline: If you are thinking about selling your home, then now is the time! ⌛ 🎯

Primary text: The market is picking up steam. Now is the time for sellers to advertise their properties. Avoid common pitfalls by connecting with the appropriate people and selling your property at the right price.

Ad copy 23

Headline: Enhance the chances of selling your home at the right price!

Primary text: When it comes to selling a home, not everyone gets it right. If you make the mistake of not listing your home and instead put it on XYZ platform (where it's just another option among many others) you say goodbye to your chances of getting something extra. It's better to list your home with professionals who will present it to the right people and bring you the best deal.

Ad copy 24

Headline: 🏠💲😊 Find your home's accurate market value with just a few clicks.

Primary text: Your home's value doesn't have to be a mystery anymore. You can get the most accurate numbers by logging on to our website and putting in a few details. Log on now and find out your home's actual value.

Ad copy 25

Headline: ✓ 💧 🉐 🏠 Getting the best value for your home has never been this easy!

Primary text: With the help of listings and advertisements on social media, real estate professionals can sell your home for the best value now more than ever. Then, as interest builds in your home, competition is created. We don't budge when it comes to selling for the right price. Get in touch with us at www.____ to sell your home.

Ad copy 26

Headline: ☹️ ☹️ 💲 🏠 Confused about how much your home is worth in the current market?

Primary text: With our knowledge and expertise, your home's current value won't be a mystery anymore. You can provide a few details and then get an idea how much your home is worth. More importantly, we walk with you throughout the entire selling process. Log on to our website right now and get started.

Ad copy 27

Headline: 🉐 💧 🏠 Homeowner, we have fair offers and faster ways to sell your home. What do you say?

Primary text: For homeowners looking to sell their homes at the right price, we have buyers willing to purchase them. With no extra closing fees and quick offers, you'll love how we get amazing offers for your property. Connect with us at www.____

Ad copy 28

Headline: 🔥😱 Sell your home in ___ city while the market is red hot!

Primary text: Homeowners who are indecisive and who procrastinate listing their homes miss out on great opportunities. One has to act when the market is red hot like it is right now in ___ city. Guess what, we have serious buyers with fair offers. Get in touch with us at _____

Ad copy 29

Headline: 😱 💲❤ There hasn't been a better time to sell your home in ___ city for years.

Primary text: There isn't a situation where the market favors everyone. At times, buyers benefit because of low mortgage rates or a dip in the market. Presently, sellers are favored because of an abundance of investors in the ___ city real estate market. Get a sense of how much you can get for your home at www.___

Ad copy 30

Headline: ✔💲🏠👍 Precise market values and serious buyers for your home at www.___

Primary text: You don't have to worry about getting shortchanged on the valuation of your home. We make sure you get the best deal possible. We have serious buyers willing to take things further quickly. Fill out the form and get the listing process underway to sell your home. Let us help you get the best price. Get in touch with us at www.___

Open House Ad copies

A real estate open house allows potential buyers to walk through the property before they decide whether to make an offer. Since most of us would not be satisfied with just seeing the pictures, open houses are still popular and these ads would target serious buyers who are willing to spend something extra but always get the right deal.

Open house ad copies for BUYERS!

Ad copy 31

Headline: Exclusive list of some amazing options for you!

Primary Text: Now open! Home buyers in XYZ who have had no luck yet should contact us because our open house is now up and it will be up for the next couple of weeks. We have a list of some amazing options for you, options that will evade you in the market and you would miss out on unless you log onto www. Let us show you every hot property on the market in XYZ city. ♥ 🎯 💧 🏠

Ad copy 32

Headline: Visit and see the property in person before making a decision!

Primary Text: If you are among those who don't find pictures and videos enough and want to visit the property even before considering it let alone reaching a decision then open houses are the answer for you and we are bringing the most exciting open house for our customers in XYZ city, it will up for more than two weeks and the schedules and timings are favorable for everyone, hurry up and see the best properties on the market. 🏠 🎯 💰 🐶

Ad copy 33

Headline: Open house for properties in XYZ city!

Primary Text: Open house for properties in XYZ city! This conventional method of buying and selling properties is still very relevant and you only better your chances of selling when more serious buyers see your property, and that is possible through open houses, our previous open houses in XYZ city have been a success, and our upcoming one will last more than two weeks, but you wouldn't find the best properties available for long. Contact us at www. and get started.

Ad copy 34

Headline: Your chance to see the best properties on the market!

Primary Text: Open house for all interested!✓ 🏠 🎯 💰 Our open houses have been a success, and people have benefited from our services this time around we are even more excited to bring you the best properties in XYZ city, both buyers and sellers need to be in attendance at some point in an open house if they want to get the best deals and you can do that at www.

Ad copy 35

Headline: Get the best deal with our open houses.

Primary Text: A public event that will help you the best deal 🤝 💰 💰 ! An open house is an answer in situations where the buyers are not able to find the right property or the sellers are not able to get reach and market their property to a certain number of potential buyers, our open houses have a reputation here in XYZ city, and we strive to provide benefit to our clients, and the list of happy customers just keeps on growing, contact us at www.

Ad copy 36

Headline: Be a part of this amazing open house!

Primary Text: Buyers and sellers in XYZ city our open house for the best properties👍💯 on the market is next month, for sellers struggling to get top dollar for their property and for buyers who are finding it hard to get multiple options on the table, this is your chance to engage, be a part of this amazing public event which has helped many in the past as well, get in touch with us at ____.

Ad copy 37

Headline: Visit a long list of amazing properties listed with us!

Primary Text: A public event that benefits us all ❤😃🤝, an open house that makes it easier for everyone involved, friendly schedules, long visit hours, and more importantly a long list of amazing properties listed with us, for the community of XYZ city this is your chance to be a part of our amazing open house which will last for about __ weeks, get your listings on discussing your requirements as a buyer with one of our team members at ____.

Open house ad copies for Sellers

Ad copy 38

Headline: Struggling to find the right buyer? let us help you!

Primary Text: Attention XYZ city home sellers! If you are struggling to find the right buyer, let us help you and show your property to potential buyers through our open house event that is scheduled to occur next month. We have some serious buyers on our contact list who are eager to buy your property. Furthermore, we make sure that everyone gets a fair deal. So, contact us at _____ to get your property listed as an open house. 🎯✓💰

Ad copy 39

Headline: We can help you get a fair price!

Primary Text: Open house in XYZ city is the way to get the best money for your home. 🏠💲 This is where the buyer is at and if you are willing to sell your home, then we can help you get a fair price. All we ask is that you quickly list your home with us as we know who the serious buyers are and they usually don't wait around for long. 🏠💲🚴

Ad copy 40

Headline: Amazing opportunity to cash in on your property!

Primary Text: Attention home sellers in XYZ city! 🏠👀 This is your opportunity to cash in on your property and get a decent amount. Even if you are looking for cash offers or you don't want to pay for a lot of repair expenses before selling, we have you covered because through our upcoming open house event we are targeting some serious buyers in XYZ city for all sorts of properties across the city.

Just sold ad copies

When a potential buyer would see that a realtor has been able to sell this many properties in a city or town, then they are likely to engage if they are serious about buying a property. Just selling this many properties shows the skill, expertise, and credibility of the realtor.

Ad copy 41

Headline: Just sold near you! Find out how much did this luxury unit sell for?

Primary text: Just sold near you! How much did this beautiful luxury 4-bed unit sell for? Was this the perfect home for your family and did you miss this amazing property? Click the link to get the answers, but don't worry if you feel you have missed this amazing opportunity because we have plenty of similar options for you. Just contact us at ____ and let us help you find your dream house. 👍😀😀

Ad copy 42

Headline: Act fast because the best options don't stay around for long!

Primary text: Just sold 💲✔! A lucky buyer just bought this amazing property in ___. This is surely an amazing buy—the property was listed just over a week ago and it attracted some serious buyers. If you were one of them, then you must act fast because the best options don't stay around for long. Click to find out the price details. For queries, you can contact us at www.

Ad copy 43

Headline: An opportunity of buying your dream house!

Primary text: Just sold close to your location ❗💯🏠🏠! Search the listed homes in ... city and never miss the opportunity of buying your dream house. Fresh options are floating in the market, and you are way behind in the queue if you haven't yet made an account with us at …

Ad copy 44

Headline: Know how much your neighbor's house sold for! 🙁 🙊 🙋

Primary text: Want to know how much your neighbor's house sold for? 🙁 🙊 🙋 If you are still unaware of how much your house is worth and you don't know how to find out then check our listings, those who have sold similar houses in your area will give you the right idea of how much you can easily get for your home. Working with us is straightforward. Contact us at …

Ad copy 45

Headline: Just sold another house in your neighborhood! ✓§

Primary text: Hey, we just sold another house in your neighborhood! ✓§If you are thinking about selling your home at the right price, then we are here to help you out with our experience. We will surely get you a decent price, which is something you might not be able to achieve on your own. Contact us now and let us help you get the right price for your beautiful house. 🏠

Ad copy 46

Headline: Get top $ for your home !

Primary text: Just sold in your neighborhood. 💯! The market is gathering pace and the buyers are on their toes if you want the right price for your house then the time is now to get your house listed through us, we will ensure that your beautiful house reaches its deserving buyer who pays the right amount, why to wait another day? 🚴 ☞ Contact us right now at …

Ad copy 47

Headline: Get an idea of what sort of properties we have!

Primary text: Another beautiful property was just sold in ... city! If you are serious about buying your dream house then you cannot pass on one amazing property after another because you never know which one was meant to be the perfect one for you, check our listings at w ... and the ones that we sold recently to get an idea of what sort of properties we have and how we list them. 🏠 § 😊

Ad copy 48

Headline: Want to own a similar property? contact us!

Primary text: Our clients are having fun with us because with our previous listings and with our expertise, we have an amazing network of buyers and sellers. We sold this luxurious unit to a small family just a few days back and if you want to own a similar property, then contact us at www.

Ad copy 49

Headline: Get the right price for your house!

Primary text: Your neighbors got top dollar for their house. § 🏠 ✓ ❤ We have recently sold some amazing properties in your area and we have helped our clients get top dollar for them. If you are confused about the actual worth of your house and you are struggling to get the right buyer, then we are here to help you out. Through our listing, we will help you get a better reach and get the right price for your house. 🏠 💯

Ad copy 50

Headline: Can you believe that this house was sold for $...?

Primary text: Just sold for $... 😲 🎯 🏠 💲! Can you believe that this house was sold for $...? If you think your house is worth that much, but the absence of the right buyer is the only thing stopping you from selling it, then we have got you covered because we have eager buyers looking to buy your home and we are here to connect you to them. Get top $ for your home by contacting us at ...

Just listed ads

Why would just-listed ad copies work?

When a realtor has compiled a list of properties on the market and the potential buyers see it, it allows them to see the properties they would never have, plus they would also be impressed by the number of options a realtor has provided them which they might have struggled to find and when the listing is fresh it is another attraction for them that the top deals might still be available.

Ad copy 51

Headline: Here are fresh listings in your area

Primary text: Hey XYZ city 🏠, here are fresh listings in your area, and guess what some amazing deals are waiting to happen, so if you are looking to purchase a house in XYZ city and you have been waiting for the availability of options at the right price then your time has come, waste no time because the market is hot and some serious buyers are snapping up the best properties from the list, contact us at www ...

Ad copy 52

Headline: Let us find your dream property!

Primary text: # was just listed! There is only one way you can never miss the best deals and that is through our listings we have fresh listings. The best thing about our new listings is that it has an option for everyone. Whether you are into country living or you want a property in the middle of the town, we have an amazing option for you. Let us help you navigate through an amazing real estate transaction. Contact us at __ so that we can get started 👍👍!

Ad copy 53

Headline: Your dream home is on offer!

Primary text: The best homes are listed here 🏠 🎯 ✓ 👍 ! If you are not looking at our listing then you are reducing the chances of finding your dream home, we have a list of hot properties that are on offer and you should have a look and search through the best possible options we are pretty sure that we have at least a few amazing options for you, get in touch with us once you have gone through the listing and let's get the process started. We are available at www.

Ad copy 54

Headline: Ready-to-move-in properties 🏠 👌

Primary text: Fresh listings here! 💯 ✓ 🏠 👌 Ready-to-move-in properties that are on the market are listed with us and with the market getting hotter, you don't have a lot of time to keep thinking about making a decision. Log in to www ... and search through the variety of options we have for you. All we expect from you is to contact us at the right time. So, feel free to do so at www ...

Ad copy 55

Headline: Ready for a new home?

Primary text: Ready for a new home? Check out this amazing __ bed unit that is perfect for a mid-sized family. The property is in mint condition and is available for a very reasonable price. It is available since our listings are fresh, but we are getting an overwhelming number of requests for this one and similar properties. Check out our freshly listed properties that are hot on the market. 🔥 ❗ 🔥 😍

Ad copy 56

Headline: Check out the hottest properties on the market in XYZ city!

Primary text: Free list of XYZ city homes $, if you are on a house hunt in XYZ and you haven't seen our fresh listings then you are surely not looking in the right places, our listings stand apart because of the diverse options we have and we make sure that don't offer dead properties to our customers, the market is hot and each of the listed property is gaining value, log onto www. to see the fresh listings.

Ad copy 57

Headline: Fresh listings are waiting for serious buyers!

Primary text: Attention XYZ city home buyers! Your search for a new home has been made easy as our fresh listings have some hot properties which are waiting for deserving offers, if you are serious about buying a property in XYZ city then act swiftly because when the market is this hot there is no shortage of serious buyers and who knows someone might snap the house which fits perfectly for your family. 💯❤️✔️🏠

Ad copy 58

Headline: Searching for the dream home for your family?

Primary text: The housing market is on fire in XYZ city, 💧😍🏠 and our fresh listings are attracting plenty of buyers, we have made sure that the listings are diverse and the options should have something for everyone, so whether you are looking for homes on a budget or you are looking for a luxurious home which is the dream home for your family we have something for you at www.

Ad copy 59

Headline: This is your chance to buy your family home in XYZ city!

Primary text: Looking for an affordable home in the most perfect location in XYZ city? We have got you covered with our listing as we have ____ number of houses listed and you can check them out right now, none of the properties in our listings are overpriced or ones that promise more than what it offers, for serious buyers who are looking for a fair deal this is your chance to buy your family home in XYZ city at the right price. 🏠 💲 🎯

Ad copy 60

Headline: A wide range of properties to choose from!

Primary text: Hot on the market. 🔥✔ Look at the fresh local home listings that are here with us and remember that we can help you see any property that is on the market in XYZ city since the listings are fresh and only a handful of properties have gone. You still have a wide range of options to choose from, but you need to act fast because the best options don't hang around for that long! Reach out today at www. and get started. 👍 🎯 💲 🏠

Personal branding Ad copies

In any given real estate transaction, there is money involved and buyers are placing their trust in a realtor to handle their money. Buying a house is a huge event for everyone, so when a realtor has credibility and local goodwill, it would be easier for potential buyers to trust them.

Ad copy 61

Headline: Hire an experienced realtor on your side!

Primary text: The market is hot in XYZ city, and the rent prices are going up 😲 💬 🏠 🎯, get your desired property before it's gone and if you tried long and hard to get one and you haven't been successful at it then it is not just you who is at fault but your agent as well, get an experienced realtor who not only has the license but the experience at www.

Ad copy 62

Headline: Let me find you the best property on the market!

Primary text: Let me find you the best property on the market at the right price, whether it is a sale/purchase or rental transaction I have the options for you, as a realtor I have worked for so many years in this market and built a reputation which goes a long way, let me handle the transaction of your property's sale/purchase in XYZ city and know the market inside out, you should get in touch with me at ____ and get things started. 😲 🏠✔ 🏠

Ad copy 63

Headline: Let me bring you a wide range of options for buyers!

Primary text: Worried about not knowing enough about the real estate market in XYZ city? 😲 🏠 🎯 💬 don't worry because we have you covered, as a licensed realtor and someone who has built a strong social network in XYZ city, I have a wide range of options for buyers, and I have a very diverse clientele. So whether you are looking for a small family unit or want to go big on your dream home in XYZ city, we are just one call away. Contact us at ___

Ad copy 64

Headline: Have an experienced realtor with a growing reputation at your service!

Primary text: The real estate market in XYZ is very dynamic, and it changes before you know it unless you have an experienced realtor by your side you would not be able to find the best deals; both the buyers and sellers have struggled in the absence of an experienced realtor, but gladly you have an experienced realtor with a growing reputation at your service at www. 🏠 🎯 💲 👐

Ad copy 65

Headline: Let us handle the transaction for you!

Primary text: Finding hot properties in the XYZ city real estate market is a piece of cake for us, but it would surely be a nightmare for you. Let us handle the transaction because, as experienced realtors, we know the market better than you. Our team is approachable and friendly, and you can discuss your requirements at _____. Let's get things moving. 🕸️ 💧 👀 👏 💲

Ad copy 66

Headline: The right person to have by your side when buying/selling property in XYZ city!

Primary text: Do you want to buy or sell your property in XYZ city? ❤️ 💲 👏 🎯 🏠 If the answer is yes and you have struggled to find the right person, then your search would end with us. As a local realtor, I am not only focused on what comes out of your pocket because my years of goodwill and reputation have been built on providing excellent services to the good people of XYZ city. Contact me at ___ and let me help you get the best deal.

Ad copy 67

Headline: We will help you get the right deal here in XYZ city!

Primary text: If you are trying to find the right home at the right price in this current market in XYZ city, then you are in for a bumpy ride. If you have zero or little knowledge of this market, not only would you struggle to get the right price but you would also never obtain the best options. Get in touch with us at www. and let our team of experienced realtors find the best deal—which is something we do daily. Hurry up as some amazing options will get sold before you know it. $\S$ 🗔 🎯 🏠 🛵

Ad copy 68

Headline: Find the best property deal with us 🗔 ✓ $\S$ 😍!

Primary text: End your struggles of finding the best property deal with us 🗔 ✓ $\S$ 😍! With luck and market stability, anyone can strike a deal in the property market but when marketing changes overnight like it does today and with zero to little knowledge of the ever-fluctuating price, getting the right is somewhat of a challenge for people, we are aware of the market's inside out, and we have helped hundreds if not thousands of people of XYZ get the best deals when it comes to sale/purchase or even rent, logs onto www.. and let's get started.

Ad copy 69

Headline: Let the experts do what they do best!

Primary text: Are you wasting your time with a new, inexperienced realtor, when the real estate market is hot, and deals are being made left, right, and center? 😲 🏠 🗨 🛋 Remember, the best options on the market don't stay available for that long. If you stick with a realtor who has little experience in XYZ city's real estate market, then forget about doing a successful real estate transaction. Let the experts do what they do best. You can contact an experienced XYZ city's renowned realtor at www...

Ad copy 70

Headline: We will help you land the best deal!

Primary text: With extensive market knowledge and a professional network, we have got you covered when it comes to buying, selling or renting a property in XYZ city, don't think that you are going to have an easy ride and it would be a walk in the park to go through this transaction because you might not even be able to spot the problems we are capable of solving and we do it daily for our valued clients which makes them happy with our services, you can become another happy client by getting in touch with us at www.

Free webinar ad copies

Many of us don't jump into the real estate market just because of the lack of knowledge we have or the lack of time we can allot to build an understanding about it, free webinars from reputable realtors are a great way to avoid this situation, and it makes it possible for everyone to remotely get knowledge of the current market condition, and that is why more people are likely to engage.

Ad copy 71

Headline: Free webinar for home buyers in XYZ city!

Primary text: Hello to the good people of XYZ city. We are hosting a free online class to help to understand the process of buying a home. This webinar is free and all you have to do to join it is register in advance because we are getting a lot of requests. Those who have previously attended one of our sessions know what a blessing this is. Click the link below and fill up a few details to get things going. You are surely not going to regret taking some time out doing this.

Ad copy 72

Headline: Learn how to find the right property with our free webinars!

Primary text: If lack of knowledge and clear understanding of where to look and how to find the right property in XYZ city has been a stumbling block for you then we have good news for you, our webinar that is happening on 00/00/2022 is free of cost, and you are invited to join the online session, get access to exclusive content just by registering through the link and start your search for your dream home in XYZ city the right way. 🏠👊✔️💲

Ad copy 73

Headline: Free webinars for XYZ city real estate investors!

Primary text: Attention XYZ city real estate investors! Our free webinar is happening this weekend, and if you are jumping into the real estate industry as an investor, then this is the best platform for you to educate yourself on the current market, get expert advice and find answers that have evaded you to date. We invite you to join us this ___ at __ pm sharp. 😯💰👍🏠

Ad copy 74

Headline: [Free webinar] Discover how to find the best deals quickly

Primary text: Our free webinar is happening on ___ at __ pm and you wouldn't want to miss out, we are educating investors and the general public of XYZ on the current market and how to get the best deals, and what to avoid when doing a real estate business transaction in the current market, the best thing about it is that it is free and all we require is to fill up a form and get yourself registered, click the link below to get yourself registered right now. 🏠👍💰✓💯

Ad copy 75

Headline: Discover How to invest in XYZ city's real estate market effectively!

Primary text: Want to learn about investing in XYZ city's real estate industry remotely? Not everyone has the time and energy to visit realtors every week just to educate themselves about the current market and honestly, the realtors don't have the time to brief each person on what's going on. Our free webinars are designed to help people searching for exclusive information on the current real estate market in XYZ city, so click the link below and get registered now. ❗👉😊💧🏠

Ad copy 76

Headline: Free remote learning for first-time buyers in XYZ city!

Primary text: Buying your first home in XYZ town? Learn how to save money and get the deal on the right price with expert advice, we are remotely teaching the general public how to look for the right property and what filters to put in, our webinar which is an online class is happening on ___ at ___ pm and you are invited to join it, registered now by clicking the link below and avoid any late entry issues. 💥 😦 😑 🏠 ✔

Ad copy 77

Headline: Build an understanding of the basics as an investor!

Primary text: There are a lot of things that you need to take under consideration when buying a home in XYZ city right now, there is a lot about the market that can change overnight, and just the thought of it is frightening especially for new investors, what we are doing about it is that we are hosting a free online class, this webinar is taking place this weekend, and we already have some people on board. You can click the link below and get yourself registered right now. ✔ 🏠

Ad copy 78

Headline: Attend this before buying your first home

Primary text: Attention first-time home buyers in XYZ city, there is so much more pressure on the buyer to get it right when the market is hot and it leaves zero or very little margin of error, educate yourself on what you need to consider when buying your first home in XYZ city through our online class, our webinar helps you build an understanding of what's required of you and you are better equipped to do a better deal, follow the link mentioned below to get yourself registered. 👆 🏠 💲 🆕

Ad copy 79

Headline: Understand XYZ city real estate market in no time!

Primary text: Want to learn about the XYZ real estate market in no time? A lot of people have benefitted from our free webinar, this free online class has come to a blessing for those who want to remotely learn all about the current real estate market in XYZ city, you are invited to join our webinar which is happening this __day at __ pm, hurry up and register yourself for the best free webinar on the internet on this topic. 😃 💲 🏠 👆 💯

Ad copy 80

Headline: Get your real estate questions answered!

Primary text: Is it the worst time to invest in XYZ city real estate right now? Are you making a mistake selling your property right now? Have you put the wrong asking price for your property? What is the reason behind not getting a decent number of responses from potential buyers? Get the truth and all the answers to these questions by going to our free webinar. You don't even have to take out a dollar from your pocket as our webinar is free. So, register now by clicking on the link below. 😃 💲 🏠 ✓ 🤑

Free buyer guide or buyer report ad copies

New home buyers have a tough time finding the right deal and most of us don't have the time or energy to learn everything about buying a home before we start our search. A buyer's guide helps new buyers make our lives easier, and when a realtor can provide one for free, then it would do a lot of good to their reputation, and more people would contact them.

Ad copy 81

Headline: Free buyer's guide for XYZ city home buyers!

Primary text: XYZ city home buyers, this is your chance to learn all about the current market situation in XYZ city and learn that there are a handful of things that you need to do as a buyer. I will be happy to be your buying guide and help you land the home of your dreams in XYZ city. Simply follow my page to get the best advice about your purchase. 💲😀💯

Ad copy 82

Headline: Get ahead of the competition with our free buyer's guide for XYZ city!

Primary text: Home buyers in XYZ city! We have created a free guide for you, which has some tips to help you avoid the mistakes that people commit when buying a home. Take some time out to read our report and avoid the mistakes and you will thank us later. Click to get the guide right now. 🎯💰

Ad copy 83

Headline: The best free guide for buyers has been put together by our experts!

Primary text: Attention XYZ home buyers! Our team of experts has put together an amazing guide for new buyers here in XYZ city, if you are thinking about how to get the best deals even if you don't have a lot of extra money to pay then this guide will help you greatly, we have educated people on how to find the right deals at the best price, and you can also do that for free, click to get our free buyer's guide.

Ad copy 84

Headline: You'll have a hard time without our free buyer's guide for XYZ city!

Primary text: Doing a successful real estate transaction in today's market is very hard when you don't have an experienced realtor with you. However, not everyone has access to a highly paid-service provider. The good news is that you have our free buyer's guide that is meant to help new home buyers in XYZ city. Just click on the link below to get our free buyer's guide and get things going. [NEW] 🤞✓

Ad copy 85

Headline: Nobody is offering an extensive free buyer's guide like we are!

Primary text: Start earning money in XYZ city's real estate industry with our free home buyer's guide, which our team has put together after a lot of thought and discussion. It covers all the major aspects of buying a home in XYZ in the current market. Follow the tips and guidelines and you'll never go wrong with XYZ home buying. Our guide is free of cost—get it now at _____. [NEW] 👉💲🎯🏠

Ad copy 86

Headline: We have the best free buyer's guide on offer!

Primary text: There are millions of licensed realtors in the country and XYZ city also has an abundance of realtors, so finding the best one within a given timeframe would be a challenge, you could take your time in finding the one that suits you but waste no time in educating yourself on how to buy your first home in XYZ city, you can do that through our free buyer's guide that is on offer and it has been helping people a lot in saving thousands of dollars, you can get for free at ___.

Ad copy 87

Headline: Free home buyer's guide for first-time home buyers

Primary text: First-time home buyers in XYZ city would find it tricky to get everything right when making the first purchase, whether you are buying your dream home which is ready to move in or you want to enter the real estate market as a small investor, this is your chance to learn everything about it for free, click on the link below 👉🏠💲⊚ and get a copy of our buyer's guide which has some really important information on the current market for buyers in XYZ city.

Ad copy 88

Headline: Download our extensive buyer's guide for XYZ city!

Primary text: Is it the worst time to buy a property in XYZ city? Is it a seller's market right now? Are you about to overpay for the home you are buying in XYZ city? Are you on the verge of buying a dead property that will be hard to sell? Get answers to all these questions from an expert through our XYZ city buyer's guide which is available for free at 👉 __. ⊚💲

Ad copy 89

Headline: Extensive free buyer's guide for home buyers.

Primary text: Has your search for a home in XYZ city been unsuccessful? Are you struggling to find the right property despite having the resources? If the answer is yes then the solution to this is our free buyer's guide which is a blessing for XYZ home buyers, especially the first-time buyers who have followed our guidelines and have been able to do excellent deals, we have compiled all the information you need and you can get your free digital copy of our free buyer's guide at _____.

Ad copy 90

Headline: Get expert help through our buyer's guide

Primary text: Are you thinking about buying a new home in XYZ city? Before you set upon the search for a home in XYZ city ask yourself the question of whether you have gathered enough information as a new buyer. Do you know what to do when you hit a roadblock? Because for many of us, buying a new home in XYZ in the current market isn't that simple. Get expert help through our buyer's guide at ___. 🛍️💯✅🏠

Free seller guide or seller report ad copies

Even in a seller's market, people find it hard to get the right money due to their lack of understanding and the mistakes they make. When a local realtor goes the extra mile and provides home sellers in XYZ city with a guide on how to sell the house for the right money and that clearly outlines the mistakes sellers should never commit, sellers will be more likely to engage with them.

Ad copy 91

Headline: A free seller's guide which helps XYZ city sellers!

Primary text: 2022 projections, Real estate opportunities and expectations for sellers in XYZ city ⚡🎲💰 if you want to cash in on your property then the time is now and before you list any of your property then go through our free selling guide and make sure that you are valuing your property correctly, get a digital copy of our seller's guide free at ___. 💰✓🏠💲

Ad copy 92

Headline: Free seller's guide for XYZ city sellers!

Primary text: Our free seller's guide will help you through a step-by-step process to profitably sell your home in XYZ city, our guide has been such a hit among the new seller as this has not only given them the right education on how to cash in on your property but it has done it free of cost, you can get a copy of our free seller's guide at _ and get things started. 💲🏠✓💰🎲

Ad copy 93

Headline: Get the best deal as a new home seller!

Primary text: The real estate market is changing in XYZ city, and as a current seller, you need to keep yourself updated, download our free seller's guide to get a detailed view of today's market and ensure that you get the best deal as a new seller in XYZ city, click the link to buy to download our updated free of cost seller's guide now. ✓ 🎯 ▯

Ad copy 94

Headline: Free seller's guide for XYZ real estate market!

Primary text: It's the seller's market and if you are still not getting top dollar for your property, then you are doing something wrong. Is it the valuation? Is it the reach? Or is there something with the property itself that needs changing? Get all answers through our extensive seller guide for XYZ state's real estate market right now. Click the link below to get a copy of our free seller's guide right now. 🎯 ✓ 💲 🏠

Ad copy 95

Headline: Ready to sell your home? Read our free seller's guide for XYZ city!

Primary text: If you are ready to sell your home and you want to avoid the common mistakes that sellers make then click the link below to get our free-of-cost seller's guide, the XYZ city's seller community has learned a lot through our free webinars and now we have come up with this amazing guide which is free for you, download it now through the link given below. 👉 🎯 ✓ 💲 🏠

Ad copy 96

Headline: [Free Seller Guide]Get top dollar for your home!

Primary text: Attention home sellers in XYZ city! If you are about to sell your home and you have not yet given read our free seller's guide, then you might make some common mistakes that are going to cost you a lot of money. Download our seller's guide for free now and get the tips you need to avoid these mistakes. Click the link below now. ❗💲👍

Ad copy 97

Headline:Don't have the right knowledge when selling your home?

Primary text: Do you think that the buyers would easily bring some extra cash to the table? Do you think it is easy to get top dollar for your home just because the market is hot? If you think like this, then you are mistaken because many important things make a difference. We are here to tell you all about it through our free seller's guide. Get a copy right now by clicking the link below. 💲❗👍🏠 🎯

Ad copy 98

Headline: Now is the time to educate yourself through our free seller's guide!

Primary text: XYZ city's real estate market is for sellers and it favors them. This is what you must have heard from a lot of people but do you know the reason why so many of the sellers are still unable to get a decent amount for their property? The reason is the common mistakes that sellers commit but you can avoid that by reading our seller's free guide, get your free copy right now by clicking on the link below. 🎯🏠❗💲

Ad copy 99

Headline: Save thousands of dollars with our free seller's guide for XYZ city!

Primary text: Attention home sellers in XYZ city! New and regular sellers commonly commit mistakes that cost them thousands of dollars, the market is full of experienced buyers who know how to negotiate and bring your property's value down and if you don't know how to tackle that then forget about getting the deserving amount for your property, our seller's guide for XYZ city home sellers is the perfect way to educate yourself on the topic and by following these guidelines you will keep yourself away from making such mistakes, download the free sellers' guide right now. 🏠👌§

Ad copy 100

Headline: Avoid common selling mistakes through our free seller's guide for XYZ city home sellers!

Primary text: XYZ city's current real estate market favors the sellers! It is a seller's market right now! These are some of the common statements that you must have heard when you mention selling your home. However, in reality, not everyone is getting a decent amount for their home even though there is an influx of serious buyers here because the market never favors the buyer or seller—it favors the one who has all the right information about the current market status. The good news is that you can get the right information for free through our XYZ city's seller's guide. Download a copy right now by clicking the link below. 👉✓🎯🏠§

DONE-FOR-YOU CAMPAIGN SETTING

Campaign Objective

For landing page conversions, use conversions objective. Make sure the Facebook pixel is correctly integrated and events are set as lead generation.

You can use software like Clickfunnels to build a landing page quickly.

Also, be sure to go to https://soldouthouses.com/templates/ to get access to our landing page templates.

If you don't have a landing page, and you would like to generate leads with a Facebook form, start with the campaign objective set as lead generation. It is important to select a special ad category such as housing and select the correct region. It will not be approved by Facebook otherwise. (See attached.)

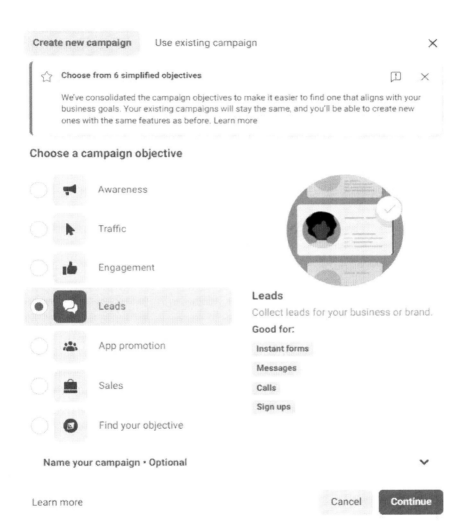

Campaign name

ℹ More options for name templates

New Leads Campaign

Create template

Special Ad Categories

Declare if your ads are related to credit, employment or housing, or about social issues, elections or politics. Requirements differ by country. Learn more

Categories

🏠 Housing ▼

☐ 🖊 **Credit**
Ads for credit card offers, auto loans, long-term financing or other related opportunities.

☐ 💼 **Employment**
Ads for job offers, internships, professional certification programs or other related opportunities.

☑ 🏠 **Housing**
Ads for real estate listings, homeowners insurance, mortgage loans or other related opportunities.

☐ 📢 **Social Issues, elections or politics**
Ads about social issues (such as the economy, or civil and social rights), elections, or political figures or campaigns.

Campaign details

Buying type
Auction

Campaign objective ℹ
Leads

Show more options ▾

Ad Set Level

Here you select demographics, allocate budget, and select the audience.

Budget

For a budget, start with $10/day. You can scale it later once you have a winning ad set.

Audience

For a targeted campaign, the optimum audience size is 100k – 500k, which can be achieved by narrowing the audience. (See attached.)

The key here is to try using different ad sets for testing, identify a winning ad set, eliminate other ad sets, and increase the budget of the winning ad set.

Once you have identified a winning ad set, don't change it. Instead make duplicates and try to enhance the winning ad set by making changes and testing.

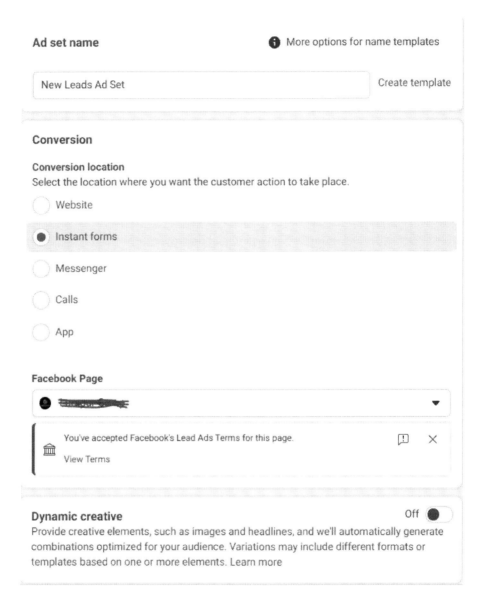

Ad set name   ⓘ More options for name templates

New Leads Ad Set   Create template

Conversion

Conversion location
Select the location where you want the customer action to take place.

○ Website

● Instant forms

○ Messenger

○ Calls

○ App

Facebook Page

● ▬▬▬▬▬   ▼

🏛 You've accepted Facebook's Lead Ads Terms for this page.   ⬛! ✕

View Terms

Dynamic creative   Off ⬤
Provide creative elements, such as images and headlines, and we'll automatically generate
combinations optimized for your audience. Variations may include different formats or
templates based on one or more elements. Learn more

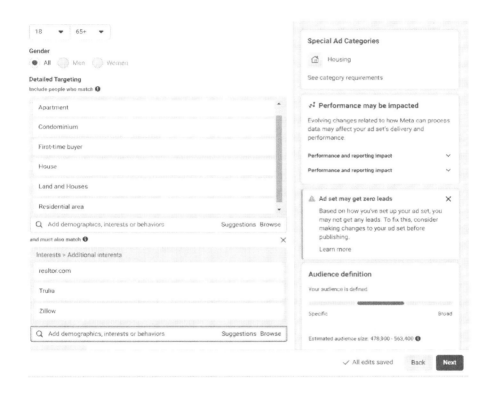

Targeting

Find below my winning set of audiences.

Audience Set A (General Buyers)

Apartment, condominium, first-time buyer, land and houses, townhouse, single-family detached, terraced house, penthouse, home automation, modern architecture, luxury vehicles, real estate investing & residential area

Narrow it down to:

Market places such as Zillow, Trulia, and Realtor.com

Audience Set B (House or Apartment Specific)

Apartment, condominium, first-time buyer, penthouse, home automation, modern architecture, real estate investing, luxury vehicle & residential area

Replace apartments with townhouses, single-family detached, and land and houses when targeting housebuyers.

Narrow it down to:

Market places such as Zillow, Trulia and Realtor.com

Audience Set C (Home Sellers)

Land lot, land and houses, modern architecture, renovation, moving company, buy to let, financial services, home repair, investment management, Trulia, investment strategy, real estate development, interior architecture, property management, construction, home automation, real estate appraisal, asset management, real estate investing, wealth management, homeowner association, home construction, Zillow or return on investment

Narrow it down to:

Reverse mortgage, home equity loan, cash out refinancing, home equity line of credit, loan, home equity, refinancing or pre-qualification (lending)

Ad

At this level, add creatives and use eye-catching primary texts and headlines. Use Facebook's multiple primary text and headlines option and add at least 3 each for better results. Leave the placement to auto.

See below:

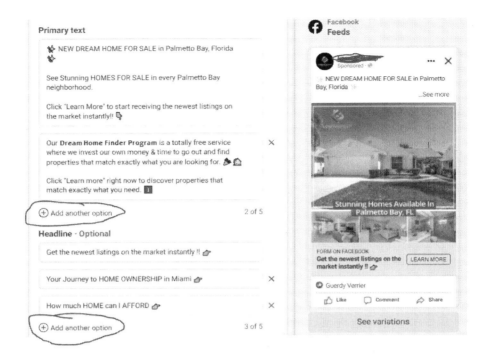

Primary Text Example 1

Our **Dream Home Finder Program** is a totally free service where we invest our own money & time to go out and find properties that match exactly what you are looking for. 🎉 🏠

Click "Learn more" right now to discover properties that match exactly what you need. ↴▫

Primary Text Example 2

🎋 NEW DREAM HOME FOR SALE in Palmetto Bay, Florida 🎋

See Stunning HOMES FOR SALE in every Palmetto Bay neighborhood.

Click "Learn More" to start receiving the newest listings on the market instantly!! 👇

Primary Text Example 3

 Looking for your dream home?

New Alexandria, VA homes starting from the high $700s.

We use our experience to provide guidance & support throughout the buying process, from personalizing your home to connecting you with the right lender for your needs.

Click "Learn more" right now to discover properties that match exactly what you need. ⤵☐

Headline Examples

- Get the newest listings on the market instantly!! ☐
- Your Journey to HOME OWNERSHIP in Miami 👉
- Your DREAM HOME in Palmetto Bay, Florida 👉

Always Be Testing:

Make sure you test your campaigns at each level. Use multiple ad sets, multiple images, and different texts. Test one variable at a time to measure results more accurately.

Get Our Done-For-You Landing Page Templates

I highly recommend you send traffic to a landing page instead of using Facebook's lead generation ads to generate leads.

My go-to landing page builder is Clickfunnels, which is easy-to-use, powerful marketing software. You can go to https://getCFfreetrial.com to get a free trial.

You can also go to https://soldouthouses.com/tempate to get access to your landing page templates & setup guide.

SPECIAL BONUS

Would You Like Our Team to Design a Custom Marketing Plan for Your Real Estate Business - for Free? Thanks for making it to the end; I hope you have enjoyed this book so far.

Now, you have more ideas to generate more leads online.

And you may also want some expert opinions on what to do next.

That's why I want to provide you with a free one-on-one strategy call.

What you are going to get:

One of our marketing experts will meet with you live (using Skype or phone) and design a customized marketing plan specifically for your real estate business.

Once it's designed, we'll then build you a blueprint and a process map, so you'll be able to deploy it at will.

Here's How it Works

We begin working before we ever meet.

First, you must complete an application form and tell us about your business.

We analyze your target market, spy on your competitors, and play "mystery prospects" by going through your website, fan page, and content as if we were potential prospects.

Then We Meet, One-On-One.

We'll do it using Skype or phone,

and we will discuss the things that need to be changed to attract more high-quality leads.

Again, everything is custom and explicitly designed for your business after we've asked you about your marketing process, revenue goals, and branding strategy.

There Is No Charge for This, and There Is No Catch.

... This, of course, leads you to wonder, *"Why would he do all of this work for free?"*

Well, this is how I get clients in the interest of full transparency.

A good percentage of the people I do this for end up asking me to manage their social media, build their websites and their sales funnels, write all their content, and set up their marketing campaigns.

When that happens, my team and I set up their account, build all the web pages, build the follow-up campaigns, write the content, set up ads and implement everything for the client.

So, that's my "hidden motivation" for doing this. However ...

This Is NOT

A "Sales Pitch in Disguise"

Far from it.

You'll get no pressure to become a client because we let the value of the free work speak for itself.

For free, the marketing plan we design for you will be absolutely transformational for your business.

I guarantee it.

The bottom line is that we'll design you an amazing marketing plan for free, and we'll even give you a blueprint of it so you can deploy it at once.

After that, you might want to become a client. Or not.

I won't pressure you either way.

If you'd like a free, customized marketing plan and blueprint, click the link below to get started.

Go to

http://soldouthouses.com/call

to book your free strategy call.

RESOURCES

Thanks for taking this book; the following are some resources that can help you take your real estate business to the next level

1. The Ultimate Real Estate Marketing Checklist (Free)

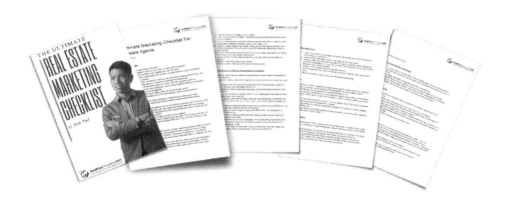

Get 86 proven real estate marketing ideas
to generate more leads online

please go to https://soldouthouses.com/checklist
to download your free checklist

2. Sold Out Houses Pro Membership

You can also join our pro membership to get access to over 1700+ real estate marketing tools & templates for only a few bucks a day.

Go to https://soldouthouses.com/vip/
to learn more about this special package

3. Our Digital Marketing Services

Want my team to take care of your internet marketing for you?

Visit Our site at https://services.soldouthouses.com/ to see what you can do to bring your real estate marketing to the next level

4. 150 done-for-you real estate infographics

Get your social media content ready in the next few minutes.

You can get your infographic package at
https://soldouthouses.com/infographics.

5. 360 real estate social media post templates

Create professional social media content
quickly with those templates

You can get those templates at
https://soldouthouses.com/socialmediaposttemplates

6.360 real estate ad templates

Create professional social media ad images
quickly with those templates

You can get all templates at
https://soldouthouses.com/adtemplates

7. Free 10X Leadgen Bootcamp

Discover how to generate more leads with digital marketing with our free virtual bootcamp

Sign up for free at https://soldouthouses.com/10xleadgenbootcamp

Made in the USA
Coppell, TX
10 November 2022

86134086R00042